D1572675

THALASSA: ONE WEEK IN A PROVINCETOWN DUNE SHACK

Also by Allen Young

Out of the Closets: Voices of Gay Liberation, editor, with Karla Jay, Douglas-Links Books, 1972. Twentieth anniversary edition issued in 1992 by New York University Press.

After You're Out: Personal Experiences of Gay Men and Lesbian Women, editor, with Karla Jay, Links Books, 1974.

Gay Sunshine Interview with Allen Ginsberg, Grey Fox Press, 1974, also published in translation in Spain, Italy, France, Brazil and the Czech Republic.

Lavender Culture, editor, with Karla Jay, Jove Books, 1977, new edition from New York University Press, 1994.

The Gay Report, with Karla Jay, Summit Books, 1977.

Gays Under the Cuban Revolution, Grey Fox, 1981. Spanish-language edition published in Madrid, Spain.

More Than Sand and Sea: Images of Cape Cod, editor, with wood engravings by G. Brender à Brandis, The Brandstead Press, 1982, facsimile edition by Millers River Publishing Co., 1985.

North of Quabbin: A Guide to Nine Massachusetts Towns, Millers River Publishing Co., 1983.

The Millers River Reader, editor, Millers River Publishing Co., 1987.

North of Quabbin Revisited: A Guide to Nine Massachusetts Towns North of Quabbin Reservoir, Haley's, 2003.

Erving Paper Mills Centennial, 1905-2005, Erving Paper Mills, 2005.

Twenty Years, Twenty Hikes: A Guide to Twenty Hikes on Protected Land in North Central Massachusetts, with John Burk and Elizabeth Farnsworth, Mount Grace Land Conservation Trust, 2007.

Make Hay While the Sun Shines: Farms, Forests and People of the North Quabbin, iUniverse, Inc., 2007.

THALASSA

ONE WEEK IN A

PROVINCETOWN
DUNE SHACK

ALLEN YOUNG

Haley's
Athol, Massachusetts

Haley's

488 South Main Street

Athol, MA 01331

haley.antique@verizon.net

800.215.8805

Cover design by Bachner+Co

With thanks to Mary-Ann DeVita Palmieri.

International Standard Book Number: 978-1-884540-23-3

Library of Congress Catalogue Number: 2010929789

in memory of

Roger Beatty

1950-2007

Contents

Illustrations

The author on the Thalassa deck near the "good luck" horseshoe mentioned on page 41

A Unique Cottage at the Seashore

One day in the spring of 2007, I received word that I had won the lottery. This lottery didn't involve any money but rather an opportunity to stay for one week in a Provincetown dune shack.

The good news came in a letter from the Peaked Hill Trust, based in Provincetown at the far end of Cape Cod, Massachusetts. The trust is a small non-profit organization that manages some of the historic shacks under an agreement with the Cape Cod National Seashore (CCNS).

Thalassa: One Week in a Provincetown Dune Shack contains the full text of a journal I kept during my stay there, August 25 to September 1, 2007. The journal has been edited, but only slightly, to make it more comprehensible to the reader.

There are nineteen dune shacks in an area known as the Dune Shacks of the Peaked Hill Bars Historic District. The status of these shacks is complicated and has been a subject of debate and uncertainty ever since the National Seashore itself was created in 1961. Administered by the United States Department of the Interior's National Park Service, the CCNS encompasses 43,500 acres of ponds, woods, and beach frontage. It includes nearly forty miles of seashore along the Atlantic-facing eastern edge of Cape Cod including much of the land in the towns of Provincetown, Truro, Wellfleet, Eastham, Orleans, and Chatham.

In my view, the protection of this precious resource is the most important legacy of John F. Kennedy (1917-1963), the nation's 35th president, a Massachusetts native who knew Cape Cod well and loved it immeasurably.

photo by Allen Young

Dunescape in the shack district

Legislation creating the CCNS was introduced in Congress in 1959 by the United States senators from Massachusetts, Kennedy and Leverett Saltonstall, but when it was signed into law by President Kennedy two years later, not everyone was celebrating. There were those who wished to make money from development of the land—similar to development that was occurring and continues to occur in so many coastal areas of the United States. The developers' wishes were thwarted. Instead, the federal government has provided public access to this place in perpetuity for millions of people from around the world.

Located along a strip of about three miles of land between Race Point in Provincetown to High Head in Truro, the dune shacks were certainly an oddity that on some level was seen as interfering with the natural beauty of the dunescape.

Henry David Thoreau described the terrain in his 1865 book, *Cape Cod:*

> From the first high sand-hill, covered with beach-grass and bushes to its top, on the edge of the desert, we overlooked the shrubby hill and swamp country which surrounds Provincetown on the north, and protects it, in some measure, from the invading sand. Notwithstanding the universal barrenness and the contiguity of the desert, I never saw an autumnal landscape so beautifully painted as this was. It was like the richest rug imaginable, spread over an uneven surface; no damask nor velvet, nor Tyrian dye or stuffs, nor the work of any loom, could ever match it.

It was quite logical that some conservationists, including people associated with the US Department of the Interior, wanted to have this place return to the most natural, undisturbed condition possible. For example, those with a vision focusing on the pristine natural world wanted to put an end to motor vehicles driving on the beach for fishing and other forms of recreation.

However, local people as well as regular visitors, while realizing they had to accept federal authority, pressed on with the desire to maintain old Cape Cod traditions. Over time, therefore, compromises were made and the National Seashore set up a permit system for limited access for such vehicles. This explains the beach vehicular traffic that I mention in my journal, which seems to be a contradiction to the conservation ethic. And so it was with the dune shacks, equally man-made, and in the view of some, another sort of pollution.

The dune shacks have a long history and a contemporary constituency—people who use them and care about them, including individuals like me. The first dune shacks were erected by men working in the Life Saving Service, precursor to the Coast Guard, probably for use by seamen they rescued or by family members who came out into the dunes for short-term visits. The shacks were never residences for the Life Saving Service staff itself.

A Coast Guard document from the late 1800s, when a life-saving station was built, states:

> A more bleak or dangerous stretch of coast can hardly be found in the United States than at this station. The coast near the station rightly bears the name "ocean graveyard." Sunken rips stretch far out under the sea at this place, ever ready to grasp the keels of the ships that sail down upon them, and many appalling disasters have taken place here. There are two lines of [sand] bars that lie submerged off the shore . . . these bars are ever shifting.

Two documents prepared by CCNS ethnographers provide the most detailed discussion of the dune shacks, and they can both be found on the CCNS web site, http://www.nps.gov/caco. The documents are *Dwelling in the Dunes: Traditional Use of the Dune Shacks of the Peaked Hill Bars Historic District, Cape Cod* (2005), by Robert J. Wolfe and *Traditional Cultural Property As-*

sessment: Dune Shacks of the Peaked Hill Bars Historic District, Cape Cod National Seashore (2006), by Robert J. Wolfe and T.J. Ferguson.

The first shacks were probably built in the late 1800s and early 1900s, using bits of lumber and other materials that washed up on the shore. It's doubtful if any of these original shacks survive.

In 1989, an area of fifteen hundred acres was designated the Dune Shacks of the Peaked Hill Bars Historic District, and supporters who wanted to protect the shacks overcame opposition from the Cape Cod National Seashore and were successful in having the district declared eligible for inclusion in the National Register of Historic Places. The Keeper of the Register described the dune landscape as "the linchpin of the district's cultural importance" while also noting that the

> shacks' unpretentious, predominantly one-room structure, their simple materials and craftsmanship, their mobility, and their lack of amenities such as electricity and running water enabled their inhabitants to experience a survivalist relationship with nature.

The Keeper added:

> The dune shacks and the dunes themselves represent a historic cultural landscape comprised of a distinctive, significant concentration of natural and cultural resources united by their shared historic use as a summer retreat for the Provincetown colony of artists, writers, poets, actors, and others. The importance of the dune shacks is embodied in their collective association with the historical development of the arts, their Spartan utilitarian form, and their unique relationship with the harsh dune environment.

In *Dwelling in the Dunes*, Wolfe describes the shacks as

> small, weathered, and rustic looking, built on skids or pilings allowing for occasional repositioning on unstable

dunes. Minimal infrastructure typified the "fragile house type," purposely designed to accommodate a fluid and relatively unspoiled natural environment. Shacks survive harsh conditions through unending maintenance and small adjustments by shack residents, including low-tech methods of sand management using simple sand fences and dune plants.

Tackling the cultural issue, Wolfe writes:

> At least three identifiable traditions find expression in the cultural pattern of temporary dune dwellers. First, some dune users are identified with "Old Provincetown," Backshore [the oceanfront area, as opposed to the village and harbor on the bay side] traditions including salvaging, foraging, training children, and retreating from small-town pressures. Accordingly, the dune shacks come to represent for the town iconic symbols of certain traditions perceived as threatened by outside forces. Second, the expressive traditions of the fine arts colony extend into the dunes, with shacks offering centers for writing, art, and other creative expression. Third, concepts of environmentalism associated with Thoreau and Beston find expression in the settlement as demonstrations of special relationships with Nature.

Henry Beston (1888-1968), who described himself as a "writer-naturalist" (thus much like Thoreau), was the author of an iconic Cape Cod book, *The Outermost House*, published in 1928 and chronicling his time in a rustic Eastham beach dwelling and sharing his views about the power and beauty of the natural world.

"A man may stand there and put all America behind him," wrote Thoreau about Provincetown, with no feminists teaching him to say "a man and a woman" or "a person." This "end of the earth" sensation, a simple matter of geography occasioned by Provincetown's location at the tip of a peninsula, is possibly part of what drew a fascinating assortment of people to this place where many of them were involved in what Wolfe, in his ethnographic reports, called "shack society."

While "shack society" includes ordinary families, sometimes as many as three generations that have occupied the shacks as an on-going tradition, as well as individuals like me who stay for only a week, the most interesting element has to be the array of artists and writers who came to the dune shacks for work and play throughout the twentieth century.

The idea of Provincetown as a magnet for the arts crowd may be connected to the remoteness, the availability of cheap housing and larger buildings on the wharfs for studios, the growing sense of an artistic and politically aware community, and in some cases the light that painters often crave for their work. This connection to the arts started, perhaps, in 1899 when Charles Hawthorne (1872-1930) founded the Cape Cod School of Arts. One of his relatives was Hazel Hawthorne Werner (1901-2000), and that seems to have been the point of origin of her connection to the Peaked Hill shacks, including Thalassa, which she owned for many years.

Provincetown is the kind of place that people fall in love with, and that's been the case for many decades. Mary Heaton Vorse (1874-1966), a journalist whose work reflected her feminist and leftwing viewpoint, had that experience. In 1907, she bought an old captain's house and spent much of her life there. Her 1942 book, *Time and the Town: A Provincetown Chronicle,* discusses the Peaked Hill Bars in detail.

In 1913, Mabel Dodge (1879-1962), a wealthy woman with leftwing politics, financed the Paterson Silk Workers Strike Pageant and worked on it in conjunction with John Reed, the renowned journalist played by Warren Beatty in the 1981 movie *Reds* (which includes a P-town scene). Dodge and Reed became lovers, and in 1914, they spent the early summer in P-town with Dodge buying and renovating the old Coast Guard Station at Peaked Hill Bars.

The refurbished Coast Guard Station was purchased from Dodge in 1919 by the actor-father of Eugene O'Neill as a wedding gift for his son. O'Neill's career as one of America's greatest playwrights began in the momentous summer of 1916 with the founding of the Provincetown Players and the first production of one of his plays. That same summer Reed and his new lover Louise Bryant purchased a house in P-town itself which they shared with O'Neill. Their friends, the noted gay painters Marsden Hartley and Charles Demuth, visited as guests of Reed, Bryant, and O'Neill that summer. When Reed and Bryant left for their epochal encounter with the Russian Revolution to become its first and most influential American propagandists, Reed sold the P-town house to the pioneering reproductive rights activist Margaret Sanger.

The last notable American intellectual to live in the Coast Guard Station was the renowned critic Edmund Wilson, who rented the house from O'Neill in 1927 during Wilson's first of many summers on the Cape. In one of his early diaries about life in P-town, Wilson commented on "antiques shops run by fairies." His use of a derogatory term notwithstanding, Wilson's observation is evidence of an early gay presence. The Coast Guard Station, the core around which the dune shacks were first built, was destroyed, along with many of the dune shacks, by a major storm in 1931. This storm also had an impact on the dunes, obliterating the hilly crest that gave the Peaked Hill Bars its name. Thus, there is no longer any Peaked Hill as such to climb for a view or measure for its height above sea level. Thalassa sits atop dunes that are perhaps forty feet above sea level— not nearly as high as spectacular dunes in Truro and Wellfleet. The geology of the ever-changing and fragile dunes, which I didn't give much thought to during my peaceful summer stay, is an interesting topic itself. The existence of the shacks seems to compel an interest in our fellow human beings who occupied them, thus overshadowing attention to the natural world.

Other creative people who stayed in the dune shacks include Harry Kemp (who called himself the "poet of the dunes"), Susan Glaspell, Jack Kerouac, John Dos Passos, Norman Mailer, Mark Rothko, e.e. cummings, Jackson Pollock, Jan Gelb, and Phil Malicoat.

A married couple, Tabitha Vevers and Daniel Ranalli, both artists, are perhaps representative of more recent shack dwellers. Ranalli's interesting account of the shacks is at www.berkshirefinearts.com, where a search for Ranalli will find it.

The School of Fine Arts was established in P-town in 1935 by Hans Hofmann, a refugee from Hitler's Germany, and this institution, which continued through the mid-1950s, was also important in attracting artists to the Cape. Hofmann ran a branch of his school in Manhattan, and that's where he met Jackson Pollock in 1942. Hoffman, a painter himself, was a major influence in the development of the abstract expressionist movement, and his P-town school nurtured a sexy bohemian atmosphere. Students there included the bisexual Larry Rivers and some of the more important women painters such as Joan Mitchell, Lee Krasner (Pollock's wife), and Helen Frankenthaler (the third wife of Robert Motherwell, another accomplished painter of that style and era).

A gay presence in Provincetown and around the dune shacks grew gradually, especially in the 1930s, and included summertime stays by photographer George Platt Lynes and the artist Paul Cadmus. Playwright Tennessee Williams first came to P-town in 1940, but he is better known for his connection with Key West, Florida, another "end of the road" destination with a long-lasting gay scene.

A friend of mine, Giles Kotcher, who assisted me with research for this introduction, wrote about "how and why such a remote and scenic natural spot would become a refuge for the feminists, gay men, lesbians, bisexuals, artists, writers, sexual liberationists, radical journalists and left wingers." His analysis suggested the phenomenon is connected to "the marginality of various forms of American bohemian or experimental or liberationist cliques and communities." He added:

> In order to experiment in alternative lifestyles, radically different from the American norm, one has to get away to anonymity, the anonymity of either the city or out of the city back to the far removes of nature. As in Thoreau's quotation stating that one puts all of America behind one in P-town, no American place is more liminal (a fancy deconstructionist term, pertaining to shores and borderlines between different habitats) than Cape Cod.

One of Giles's points was about me. He encouraged me to link myself to this history because of my role as a journalist active in the New Left and gay liberation movements. Such a link is made contemporary, he said, because of my involvement in the environmental movement and specifically land protection. Replying to him, I said it would be pretentious of me to suggest any personal connection to any list of famous writers and artists, but it is fair to say that whenever I do visit Provincetown, usually once or twice a year, it does involve my identity as a gay man and my intense interest in the natural world. Art, architecture, and art history are among my interests and add to P-town's allure for me.

The idea of keeping a journal came to me even before I knew that Thalassa's longtime owner was the writer Hazel Hawthorne Werner, author of *The Salt House* (1929), a memoir tracing her time amid the dunes. As soon as I knew I'd be staying at Thalassa, I was motivated to write down my thoughts, observations, and activities in a notebook because I knew I'd have a lot of time on my hands during the mostly solitary dune shack stay.

And why did I want to go in the first place? To be honest, I wanted to stay in the dune shack for the same reasons that people pay a fortune to stay in one of those luxurious Caribbean resorts where guests have their own private lodging at the edge of the sea. For my one-week stay at Thalassa, I had to pay the Peaked Hill Trust $275, less than one would pay for a single night at a seaside resort.

I knew it would be exceedingly rustic, but that didn't bother me in the least. In the 1970s, I lived without electricity or running water for several years in my then unfinished woodland home. Primarily, I was attracted to the idea of being close to undisturbed nature, sunning myself at the edge of the ocean, and swimming in the nude, the way I'm sure dune shack dwellers have done since the beginning, even though it is now against the rules. I wanted to experience quiet simplicity away from the inventions of the modern world that have most impacted my life, that is, the automobile, the telephone, and the computer.

Perhaps others stay at Thalassa with their cell phones, radios, or recorded music devices, but silence and the sounds of nature are what I usually like at home, and so it was during my week in the shack.

Let me tell you a little about my own background. I was born in 1941 in the foothills of the Catskill Mountains of New York, where my parents owned a chicken farm. The children of eastern European immigrants, Rae Goldfarb and Lou Young had intense involvement in the trade union movement and membership in the Communist Party, which meant that, like John Reed, they admired the Soviet Union. Their political fervor had a big influence on me, especially since their leftwing affiliation continued during the dangerous McCarthy era of the 1950s, my formative years.

Away from home as a student at Columbia College in New York City, starting in 1958, I developed independent thought and became involved in the fledgling New Left. While I pursued my career goals, including three years in South America where I hoped to become a foreign correspondent, I also maintained my political interests. The Vietnam War was underway and even though I had landed a coveted position as a reporter for the *Washington Post*, I felt drawn to the antiwar movement and the embryonic "underground press." I quit the Post and worked full time for Liberation News Service (LNS) from 1967 to 1970, gradually departing "the movement," as we called the New Left, in favor of gay liberation in the wake of the Stonewall Rebellion of 1969.

Lesbian writer Karla Jay and I collaborated on four books, starting with a pioneering anthology entitled *Out of the Closets; Voices of Gay Liberation*, reissued by New York University Press and remaining in print. In the spring of 1971, as political dogmatism turned me off and psychedelic drugs turned me on, I left city life with a desire to live in the country. Back-to-the-land met gay liberation with the formation of Butterworth Farm in 1973 as four friends and I purchased about a hundred acres in the rural town of Royalston, Massachusetts. Our goal was to create a gay-centered community with an emphasis on self-sufficiency.

I helped build the octagon-shaped timber-frame house where I have lived for almost four decades and where I cultivate a productive organic garden. I was a reporter and assistant editor for the local newspaper, the *Athol Daily News* and community relations director for Athol Memorial Hospital until I retired in 1999. I have written books of local interest, focusing on farms, forests, and the unique rural community of the North Quabbin

Region, and have been involved in the land protection efforts of the Mount Grace Land Conservation Trust (www.mountgrace.org).

In the journal that follows, I mention Dan Leahy, who served with me on the Mount Grace board of directors. He told me about the dune shacks after his stay there with his partner Julia Rabin and informed me how to contact the Peaked Hill Trust. I paid my twenty-five-dollar annual membership fee for five years, and each year, after entering the lottery, I got word that I was not selected. In my sixth year, I was a winner, and the journal that follows is an account of my experience. In it, there are references to Butterworth Farm and to various friends, as well as to my partner, Dave, who has been a loyal and true companion for more than thirty years although he decided not to join me at Thalassa.

So what is going to happen with the shacks? In 2007, the year I stayed at Thalassa, there was a lot of buzz about their future and even concern that tearing them down remained a possibility.

A few shacks were razed by the CCNS prior to the creation of the historic district in 1989, and there were always some CCNS personnel who disdained the shacks and their alleged value. But as I write this three years later, there seems to be no reason for such concerns. Uncertainty instead involves how the shacks will be used and how the public will benefit.

"Shack society" now includes non-profit organizations, including Peaked Hill Trust, that have managed shacks for artist-in-residence programs or lotteries for members—such as the one that got me into Thalassa. There are also long-time dune-dwelling families who continue to occupy shacks under legal agreements called "reservations of use and occupancy" and shorter term leases. In some cases, costly and contentious court battles were involved. Only one structure, the Malicoat shack, had sufficient legal documentation to assure it the status of private ownership. The other eighteen shacks are property of the United States government.

Many groups and individuals continue to play a critical role in preserving the shacks and the associated landscape and natural environment. The National Park Service has ultimate responsibility of ensuring that this National Register property is preserved. In a conversation with Sue Moynihan, Chief of Interpretation and Cultural Resources Management of the CCNS, I learned that since 1989, the historic district has been eligible for the National Register, and "the National Park Service has been treating it as though it is listed." The final research and documentation to list the district is underway and should be completed in 2010. The ethnographers who prepared the 2006 *Traditional Cultural Property Assessment,* Robert J. Wolfe and T.J. Ferguson, recommended that the shacks receive additional National Register significance as a traditional cultural property. However, the Keeper of the Register determined that the district did not meet the criteria for this additional area of significance. This was a disappointment for some in shack society, but the ruling seems to me to be mostly a technicality that does not undermine the shacks' future.

A National Environmental Policy Act environmental assessment is underway with plenty of opportunity for public input. "Continued public access to the district's themes and resources will be an outcome of this planning process," Moynihan concluded.

Dr. Carol Carlson, executive director of the Peaked Hill Trust (PHT), replied by email as follows to a question I posed while writing this introduction:

> As of now, we are at monthly meetings representing PHT at the Dune Shack sub-committee of the Cape Cod

National Seashore. Our goal is to establish a "plan" for shack use in the future. These deliberations will not be complete for at least one year. The most accurate description of where we are at this stage is "at the table with all dune shack constituencies." We are just beginning to get into discussions. After we establish one or perhaps two scenarios—the Seashore will meet and decide on shack use. Although they cannot be destroyed, thanks for the most part to PHT's membership and supporters, it is not clear what the profile of dune shack use will be.

Well, if things work out, maybe I'll get out there again and have another dune shack experience. And if you are inspired by this book, maybe you'll be competing with me in the lottery. You can contact the Peaked Hill Trust to inquire about membership: Peaked Hill Trust, Post Office Box 1705, Provincetown, MA 02657. The shack area is accessible from Route 6 where it intersects with Snail Road, and if you wander out there, don't forget to bring enough fresh water to drink. And please remember to respect the privacy of shack dwellers.

Thalassa's table with gladiolas from the author's central Massachusetts garden, kerosene lamps, candles, and the author's notebook

Thalassa on the Dunes: A Week's Journal

Saturday, August 25 - 11:45 AM: I'm seated at the table, about thirty by forty-eight inches, made of wood. I just arrived at the twelve-foot by twelve-foot cottage called Thalassa, a Greek name which means "sea." (In Greek mythology, Thalassa was a primordial sea goddess.) With weathered shingles and the trim painted light blue, and with screened windows on all sides, Thalassa is my home for a week. I already love this place with its amazing views of dunes and ocean. Soon, I'll go down the dunes on the north side and swim in the Atlantic Ocean. I see light surf and almost no people. Two families who've reached the beach with their (presumably permitted) vehicles are not far away, but that's not a lot of people—and it's mid-day on the weekend. I anticipate plenty of solitude and privacy.

Thalassa is one of four cottages or "dune shacks" managed by the Peaked Hill Trust. I joined the trust six years ago after Dan Leahy told me all about it and about his stay on the dunes located within the Cape Cod National Seashore. These old shacks are somewhat controversial because the optimum concept of the National Seashore is to have an all-natural environment, so the feds apparently would prefer to have them demolished. From what I've seen, the Trust is environmentally sensitive and does what it can to minimize the impact of visitors like me. I'll say more about this later.

Seated at the table, I'm eating a snack—a peach and some nuts. Here's what I brought for my seven days:

two peaches
a half pound of grapes
one yellow melon
a half pound of egg noodles
a half pound of bacon
six eggs

19

one steak
one chicken breast
one quart of homemade Scotch broth
one quart of yogurt
one loaf of bread
some mayonnaise
a half pound of butter
twelve ounces of mixed nuts
a half gallon of orange juice
ten tea bags
some leftover turkey meatballs and pasta
two cans tuna fish

And from my garden:
one head cauliflower
one head cabbage
a half pound of string beans
six cucumbers
three tomatoes
four potatoes
two onions

I certainly won't starve, but I expect to consume most of it. Am I compulsive about food? Maybe, but planning is important. To hike from here to the market in Provincetown, over hot dunes, would take between one and two hours each way. I don't plan on doing that.

My cousin Kip is supposed to come here from town for lunch time on Tuesday, but I'm wondering if he'll actually come and wondering if he'll find me. The many trails through the dunes are unmarked and the various shacks in our area are stretched across about a mile of dunes. We shall see.

I bought a one-time-use digital camera at CVS and took four pictures so far.

I was going to bring binoculars, but I forgot them. I don't think I forgot anything else. I brought a beach umbrella and a chair (loaned by my friend Frederick) but these items were already here provided by the Trust which also provided a gas fridge, a two-burner stove, and a bed with blankets. And there's a well nearby for potable water. Unfortunately, the Trust didn't provide me with a complete list of what I'd find at the shack.

I'm waiting for Marge, a Peaked Hill Trust volunteer who took me here in a special van with a permit and tires deflated to drive on the dune roads. She will return to give me her orientation spiel. The previous occupants left this place immaculate, and I won't have any problem doing the same for whoever follows me.

I hear the wind whistling around and through the shack and see the dune grass waving. It's time to step outdoors and sit in the Adirondack-style chairs provided for me, to take in the view and wait for Marge.

Saturday, August 25 - 1 PM: Marge returned and explained how to use the well, the outhouse, and the solar shower (hooray for all of those things). I'm going to fix myself a tuna sandwich and go for a swim.

Saturday, August 25 - 3 PM: Sun, wind, sand, and surf. How many centuries has it been just like this? OK, forget about the vehicles driving on the beach (a couple of them parked within a few hundred feet, plus about eight or so that drove by in a two-hour period). It hasn't changed that much—panorama of sky, ocean, and sand dunes—since Thoreau came to Provincetown. That was about 150 years ago.

There might be a sand bar out about one thousand yards, as I see waves breaking out there. There was a lone seagull hanging around me as I sat in my beach chair but there's nothing for it to eat. Is this bird a "regular," hanging out just below Thalassa?

photo by Allen Young

Sign for Thalassa at the foot of the path leading to the top of the dune

There were bothersome flies landing on my lower legs and biting. They are not the greenhead flies I know from Crane Beach, in Ipswich, Massachusetts, but still annoying.

One of the vehicles nearest my beach chair had three guys in bathing suits. They seemed young, but I didn't walk past them in order to get a look. I felt self-conscious to be so curious about them. Maybe I was just lazy, lounging in my chair with a book. Were they gay or straight? If I saw three guys together in a museum or at a concert, I'd think "gay." These three had fishing rods so I think "straight." One of them went swimming but only with the help of a light blue tube. That seemed a bit "sissy" to me. I'm a bit amazed at how much I succumb to stereotypes.

I wondered what it would be like for me to go on a fishing trip with my neighbor Dean and his fishing buddies? Would I actually go if invited? Probably not. I never liked fishing much. My father loved it and used to take me, but I was usually bored. Would it be different now with my power of observation so much keener and my self-esteem so much stronger? I would enjoy the experience of being out in nature and not worry at all about catching or not catching a fish.

I just looked down the beach and two of the three guys are tossing a football back and forth.

I've left the beach and am perched on the top of the dune where Thalassa is located. The breeze is constant but not enough to deter the flies. There's a clothesline with clothespins, and I hung my towel, t-shirt, and bathing suit to dry. They flap in the strong wind but seem well secured with the clothespins. At home, I hang my clothes out to dry, weather permitting, and often wonder why more people don't do it, especially in this era of awareness about energy consumption.

There's a birdhouse on a pole near the house. Somehow I don't think any birds live there. I don't seem to have any birds in the three birdhouses back home at the Octagon either.

There's a small deck on the front of Thalassa with a bench where I'm sitting now. The person who was here before me left six large bright rose hips to decorate the ledge at the edge of the deck. I won't eat them. I will try some of the beach plums Marge pointed out to me. They're down the pathway where the well is located. I'll get more water there tomorrow or the next day.

I now see *rosa rugosa* bushes on two sides of the cottage. Most of the foliage is green and healthy but there are some dying branches. There are still a few flowers but mostly I see rose hips, a fruit with seeds, really. I wonder if there's a real difference between Vitamin C with rose hips, which I usually buy for my daily intake, and just plain ascorbic acid. I guess I just assume the one with the natural ingredient is better. I also guess I don't care enough to seriously research the matter.

There's a pitcher on the table with two pink gladiolas and two yellow ones. I cut them in the garden this morning to have them here in my dune shack, transporting them with my foodstuffs, even though it was a bit difficult to do so. (I'm such a fag and proud of it. Of course, I use the term "fag" with a bit of humor, not as an anti-gay word, but to reflect a well-accepted idea about gay sensibility and the way that so many gay man appreciate flowers while for so many straight men an interest in flowers is considered unmasculine.) There's plenty of beauty here without rich showy flowers such as glads, but it adds something to the experience, and the pride in having them here is also related to the fact that I grew them.

Saturday, August 25 - 4:40 PM: I went back to the beach to take another swim. I seem to need to build my confidence about swimming here. The power of the ocean is blatantly obvious. And the vastness of it. I am the only swimmer. This is not a gentle bay, like Brewer's Bay on Tortola, British Virgin Islands, where I swam carefree last winter, or my old favorite, Sun Bay on Vieques, Puerto Rico. Nor is it the crowded beach on the Jersey shore where lifeguards control things. This beach drops off sharply, so in order to swim, you have to plunge right in. You can't walk out a bit up to your chest or neck and then swim. So it is a little scary at first.

Well, there were no warning signs about currents on the beach and no warnings in the informative booklet, *Living at Thalassa: Please Read*, provided for me here and which I read earlier today. The guy floating on his tube made me feel secure about no dangerous currents. So, I've gone in a few times and swum a bit, parallel to the shore. The water temperature is ideal, cool and refreshing but not at all icy. It eventually came back to me that I've swum before at Race Point, not far from here, and at Long Nook in Truro, essentially a continuation of this beach.

If John Fitzgerald Kennedy is to be remembered for anything, it should be the creation of Cape Cod National Seashore in the early 1960s when he represented Massachusetts in the U.S. Senate. Local real estate interests opposed its creation, but thankfully JFK was successful. He got us started defending the South Vietnamese corrupt regime (urged on by that nasty old queen Cardinal Cushing of Boston), and Kennedy's Bay of Pigs invasion was a fiasco. So, hooray for the Cape Cod National Seashore (CCNS), which protects this area from the development that has ruined much of Cape Cod.

I learned from Marge that the four dune shacks are property of the CCNS and that Peaked Hill Trust only manages them under a lease agreement. This agreement is precarious, however. Peaked Hill informs us that you may not bring your own vehicle here even if you have a permit for driving on the beach. This is due to the feds trying to minimize impact. Pets are also not allowed. There was a problem in the past with fleas, and personally I am pleased that these pet restrictions exist.

I am so pleased that the shacks are still available due to the effort of the Peaked Hill Trust. I was told that this one was built in the 1930s, I will have to buy a book to find out more history.

I only brought two beers to celebrate my first day here and the beginning of this journal, but I forgot to put them on the list I wrote earlier today. I'm going to stop writing, uncap a Yuengling lager (thanks to Nan and Leslie, who brought this brand of beer from Pennsylvania where it is brewed), and ponder the meaning of life for a while. Ha, ha.

Saturday, August 25 - 5:25 PM: All gone—the beer, that is. I also smoked some sacred herb earlier today. My friend Peter gave me a pipe he had, carved stone shaped like a penis. It was a little strange sucking on that thing, but much better than rolling a joint. I smoke rather infrequently these days, but this venue called for it.

I read a chapbook today entitled *Love & Fear: Stories and Poems* by my old friend Nick DeMartino. I enjoyed his writing, which was rather personal. Each piece was a snippet, a vignette, and some of the topics are familiar—coming out to his Mom, breaking up with a lover. (The lover wept.) Nick signed the book for me: "Allen, I'm told stories of great writers who started late. Hope springs eternal, Nick."

I enjoyed the stories and wish him well, but Nick, don't give up that nice job you have at the American Film Institute. He won't. Nick is no dummy. I've known him since the early 1970s. Ah, those special years of the continuing turmoil of the anti-war movement and the start of the gay liberation movement. Anyway, I'm glad Nick is pursuing this muse.

I am also working on some autobiographical writing in a very different style. If I ever publish it, it'll be self-published like my current new book, *Make Hay While the Sun Shines: Farms, Forests, and People of the North Quabbin*. I don't feel my writing has any commercial potential, and I don't care, either, at this point. I'm not enough of a literary critic to comment on Nick's writing. It's enjoyable to read, but I tend to like most gay auto-biographical or semi-autobiographical writing because I can relate to it.

Saturday, August 25 - 6:50 PM: I'm sitting outside, as the sun moves closer to setting. I can see a stretch of this beach about one-half mile long and there are still about ten vehicles parked on the beach. Some people are fishing. There's a family with two young boys and a girl parked below Thalassa. They are running around and seem to be having a good time. I thought this section of beach was off limits to motor vehicles, but I was wrong. Driving on the beach is a Cape Cod tradition that goes back decades before CCNS. Local people (and of course, many not local) have fought to retain their traditional use of this land. I wish these vehicles would disappear but I do understand the political battle that has been waged. This is reminiscent of land use battles out west where we've seen President Clinton's roadless policy opposed by four-wheel-drive enthusiasts who have an ally in George W. Bush. Well, I came to Thalassa in a vehicle, so I can't get on my high horse. However, I wish the dad below me would stop yelling at the kids.

It was in the eighties today, and it's starting to cool off. I took a solar shower, and the hot water felt great as the cool air blew south to north. Directions are odd here. The sun will set over land to my left as I face the ocean. A map of Cape Cod shows the way views can vary depending where you are on the "arm" that forms the geography. I'm on the north coast of Cape Cod, which is the shortest coast. It faces the ocean. The wind here, generally from the south moving towards the ocean, is different from what I would have expected: ocean breezes usually come off the ocean onto the land, not vice versa as it is here.

It's so odd to be writing by hand. I've admired beautiful penmanship, but I don't take the time to write longhand, and I don't do it often. It's fun in part because it's a rarity in today's world.

The info book for residents of Thalassa says nothing about vehicles on the beach. I wonder if they have a curfew. We shall see. It's tea time!

Sunday, August 26 - 8:45 AM: I just finished breakfast after having a good night's sleep, about ten hours. I spent a fair amount of time in the evening appreciating the solitude and watching the darkness arrive. It was very hazy, foggy, and cloudy, and there were no stars to be seen last night. The forecast was for a cloudy day today and thirty percent chance of rain, but the sun is out and the sky is hazy without any apparent cloud cover.

Breakfast consisted of two slices of bacon, one egg, one slice of bread, and tea. I didn't bring any coffee as I've been avoiding coffee for several months now to keep from having heartburn. Dinner last night included half of the leftover pasta and turkey meatballs with string beans and cucumber spears. I didn't bring any sweets with me, just some fresh fruit.

When night fell, there were still some vehicles driving with their headlights on the beach. This morning I see only one in the distance, but I'm sure more will arrive.

I miss Roger Beatty, my friend who spent so many years on the Cape as a naturalist and educator and who died at such a young age. I will be back here in four weeks for his memorial. He would have hiked in here to visit and given me the name of every plant I see, plus other environmental wisdom.

I saw some tracks in the sand this morning, probably mice scurrying about in their search for food. There are three mouse traps set in Thalassa with no bait in them. If I hear mice at night, I'll figure out a way to bait them, but last night it was quiet in here. When I awakened, as I lay in bed I felt something on my head and flicked it off. It was a spider. I grabbed a tissue to catch it or kill it, but it was faster than me. I hear about spider bites, but I'm not worried. Ticks are a variety of spiders, I think, and they are common on the Cape and Islands. I keep checking for them. So far, the small biting flies are my biggest concern.

The vegetation atop the dunes is not very complex. I see the dune grass, some sea oats mixed in, a plant that looks like the Dusty Miller in my rock garden, *rosa rugosa*, and a few other species I can't identify. I'm going to pick some beach plums later today when I go to fill the water jugs. So far I've used five gallons of water, which includes dishwashing and one shower.

I'm going to the outhouse which is quite nice, clean, and not stinky. They use some sort of composting method and haul it out after it has composted. I'm instructed to put popcorn on top of my deposits. They also use some other compost aid that looks like a mixture of wood ash and wood chips.

Thalassa's environmentally friendly outhouse

Sunday, August 26 - 9:30 AM: Just back from the outhouse. A good dump is always satisfying, and a sign of good health.

I took four empty gallon plastic jugs to the well about four hundred feet down a sandy pathway from Thalassa. In truth, all paths are sandy here. The pump is just like the pitcher pump we have at Butterworth Farm. This reminds me, I want to get that pump at home operable again. Our sixteen-foot dug well is an excellent emergency resource, but without a functioning pump, it is useless. Gathering the water here took some time and energy but was very satisfying, bringing back memories of the 1970s, when I lived at Butterworth Farm without modern plumbing.

The outhouse is about 250 feet from Thalassa, also down a sandy path. The expansive view of the open sea is spectacular this morning, the air amazingly clear. Few vehicles on the beach so far. I counted twelve sailboats or other vessels out on the horizon. It's 115 steps from the house to the beach, so in five minutes or less I can be in the ocean. This proximity is part of what makes this experience so special. Well, I washed all the dishes, and I'm going down for a walk on the beach before the arrival of too many vehicles.

Sunday, August 26 -11:00 AM: I walked west on the beach for perhaps a half mile and back. A couple of trucks went by but aside from that, the beach was deserted. There were a little bit of seaweed, some clam and crab shells, and assorted detritus: a couple of feathers, pieces of plastic, and one flip-flop sandal. Overall it was pretty clean. Oh, there was an orange peel so brightly colored. It's technically biodegradable, but on the beach, it's undesirable trash that should have been carried out by whoever ate the orange.

When I returned from the walk, I went for a swim, skinny-dipping this time as there was no one in sight.

I've regained my confidence about the ocean here; the waves are no problem because they don't break until ten or twenty feet from shore.

I ate some grapes. Their cool sweetness was much appreciated. I'm starting to feel the solitude. It is a very unusual state for me, living at Butterworth Farm with neighbors and with the telephone always present. This solitude is, so far, something I'm enjoying. Writing in the notebook is like talking to a friend, and the process of doing this makes this experience quite different from one of those silent retreats the Buddhists go on. That does not appeal to me. I don't like the idea of following someone's rules, especially religious rules.

Sunday, August 26 - 1:35 PM: Hazel Hawthorne Werner used to own this shack. Born in 1901, she was a bohemian and writer who first came to Provincetown when she was only seventeen. For many years she summered in this shack or another called Euphoria, spending winters in New York City. Like me, she was a professional writer.

The precise origin of these shacks is not clear from the book *From the Peaked Hill* that I found here. They were built some time before World War I, probably by Coast Guard personnel. Hazel bought Thalassa for seventy-five dollars. The land was already protected, state-owned, in fact, but the state was not that concerned about the assortment of some nineteen shacks on this ridge. The creation of the CCNS changed things, ending the previous informality, and introducing the possibility of razing all the shacks. The Peaked Hill Trust was formed to try to keep the shacks for public use. I can imagine the stance of the environmental purist who wants to take them down, but I'm no purist.

It's clouded up again. Before lunch, I returned to the beach. It's much less windy today, and unlike yesterday,

I could open the beach umbrella and get some needed shade while reading. I also swam again, the only one in the water. I started Cathy Stanton's book *The Lowell Experiment: Public History in a Post Industrial City.* Cathy wrote about a dozen romance novels but this is something quite different, academic writing in the field of anthropology. Her focus is on the Lowell National Historic Park, its background, function, and personnel. I visited that park about ten years ago and enjoyed it a lot. Cathy (whom I know from Athol, Massachusetts, near where I live) obviously worked very, very hard on this book. The work earned her a PhD at Tufts, but she seems about as career-oriented as I am. That is, not very.

Lunch was perfect: tuna and tomato with one slice of bread, cool cucumber spears, and lots of fresh well water.

Sunday, August 26 - 4:50 PM: I've read and napped. There's a very light drizzle now. The beach is almost deserted. One truck just drove by. None are parked. Earlier today I saw a young couple (male and female) with small backpacks. I was standing at the dune edge, and they saw me. The girl waved, and I waved back. I wanted to invite them up to show them Thalassa and make them some tea. However, inviting them up would have seemed very forced, as they were some distance from me, barely within earshot. I'm a very social person, but this dune shack experience is not social. Nor is it anti-social. It's about solitude until Kip comes, if he succeeds in getting here.

Living at Thalassa has a simple sketch showing the four Peaked Hill Trust shacks, the trails, and Jeep roads. Why wasn't I given one of these when I joined the Trust six years ago or when I won my Thalassa reservation in this year's lottery?

I've been thinking about Provincetown as a gay and lesbian mecca. Only three miles from here there are

Beer and rose hips on Thalassa's deck

hundreds, maybe thousands, of gay men and lesbians in their homes (if local) or enjoying their summer vacations. What I'm experiencing at Thalassa has so little connection to P-town as a GLBT resort. P-town's visitors are crowded on Herring Cove Beach or shopping and eating on Commercial Street. Some visitors bicycle on the paved dune trails and thus get to appreciate the dune scenery and perhaps the ecology, too. But few know about these dunes and this long unsupervised, unnamed beach. And yet, there is a connection of sorts related to the natural beauty and light, to the aesthetic experience that drew artists to P-town early in the twentieth century. Gay men and lesbians were among those artists, bohemians, and theater people who came here, and they told their friends and more came and then more. For many now, however, the attraction is more sexual, social, and perhaps cultural than aesthetic. And that's a little sad.

Sunday August 26 - 7:00 PM: The beach is deserted. I just stare at the sand and surf, the dune greenery, and a hint of pink in the cloudy western sky as sunset nears. This sight and the sound of the waves are almost hypnotic. A motorboat speeds by fairly close to the shore headed, I'm sure, for Provincetown harbor. To get there it'll go west, then south, then east, and finally west again. It's all because of the shape of the "arm" and the way it curls under itself. I love maps, and I'm so glad there's a map here because I did not bring one.

Dinner was tasty, consisting of chicken breast, cauliflower, potatoes with a little yogurt, and cucumber spears. The only seasonings I have are salt, pepper, and butter, but I've never minded plain food. Well, I should have brought some garlic anyway. Clean-up is easy as there's a large sink. Water comes out of a spigot in a large Poland Spring jug that's been modified so I can fill it with water when needed. They've supplied dish soap and assorted scrubbies. There's a nice drainer. The waste water just spills out under the shack into the sand.

I'm getting into Cathy's book on Lowell. She mentions Elkin McCallum, owner of Joan Fabrics, and the last boss of my friend Carl Miller, the talented and successful textile designer. I met McCallum with Jan Norris during the final stages of Carl's estate, for which I served as executor. Since Cathy's book came out last year, Joan Fabrics and Collins & Aikman (another firm mentioned in the book, also one that Carl worked for) have both filed for bankruptcy. Had Carl lived, I think his working environment now would be very different, and he would have had to re-invent himself. If he continued designing textiles, he'd likely be visiting mills in China.

Well, it's time for a cup of tea. I'll have it at the table where I've lit two candles and a pair of kerosene lamps. I may blow out the kerosene lamps because I don't like the fumes. I lived with such fumes for six years before I had electricity at Butterworth Farm. It's hard to fathom how I tolerated the fumes back then.

Sunday, August 26 - 7:35 PM: The western sky is so beautiful now, and the sun is gone. A short time ago I glanced up and the sun was in the window, a ball of fire. I went outside to watch the sunset. I was reminded of the first time I was on the coast of the Gulf of Mexico some time around 1990, on Anna Maria Island in Florida, where Dave and I were guests of Fred and Betty Edwards. Fred and Betty encouraged us to go to the beach to watch the sunset. There was also a sunset ritual at Mallory Pier in Key West, a place where the gay scene and the hippie scene merged in the early and mid 1970s. Here at Thalassa, when the sun was a fireball not quite set, the bright red light reflected off the tips of the dune grass, turning the dune into an unexpected light show. The sunset was a major distraction but now I'm going to have that cup of tea.

Gas fridge, lower left, and the rest of Thalassa's kitchen

Monday, August 27 - 7:35 AM: The weather has changed, and I awakened to fresh air with much less humidity. I can see things more clearly without the haze, including the huge P-town water tank and the Pilgrim Monument to my south. The other dune shacks, invisible in the haze, are now clearly seen, though tiny. These other shacks are not that close, and my original thought of perhaps interacting with, even just meeting the other shack dwellers, is no longer applicable. I've gone almost two days now not speaking to anyone. Some people talk to themselves but I'm not one of them.

The sun is already bright. The beach is deserted except for a small flock of gulls at water's edge. The waves must wash in some food for them and the other shore birds. I've seen sandpipers, perhaps. I counted nine boats out in the water, now with sails; I think there are still some working fishing boats harbored in P-town, thankfully.

I trimmed some dead blossoms off the four gladiolas and broke a few inches off the stems. They are perfectly beautiful once again. Seeing them makes me happy.

Thanks to Dave for suggesting I bring candles. I was so grateful to have them last night as I really disliked the kerosene fumes.

Monday, August 27 - 9:15 AM: The atmosphere is so different with the breeze coming offshore, the opposite of my first day here. Given the cool temperature, about seventy degrees, I decided to hike into town to leave a map and a message for Kip. He told me where he is staying, at Ainsworth Cottages, on the East End, so I should be able to find the place and either find him or leave a map and a message. I was tempted to just leave things as they are and test his ingenuity and perseverance, but I do think it might just prove frustrating for him to find me without the help of the map. So, I've had breakfast (same menu as yesterday), hauled water, visited the outhouse, and off I go from Thalassa to the outside world. I'll be back soon. I do not plan to spend time in town.

Monday, August 27, 12:40 PM: A man just walked by Thalassa and looked at me through the window. I was seated at the table eating lunch. He quickly turned away and went down the path to the beach. In the same situation, I would have said hello or sorry. And maybe added an excuse, "Just going down to the beach." The shacks are supposed to be private. The other shacks have signs that say "Private" or "No Trespassing." But there are no signs here and in any case there are very few people. This guy was the first person I've seen anywhere near the shack, except down below the dune on the beach. I was a bit startled. Before I could say anything, he was gone, which is just as well because I didn't have anything to say. *Living at Thalassa* tells me that "unwanted visitors" are sometimes a problem and that I should "feel free to firmly instruct them in dune etiquette." As relaxed and happy as I am, instructing someone in dune etiquette is not on my agenda for this week.

My walk to town this morning was very successful. On the way to town, I followed a trail that stopped being a trail so I was slightly disoriented, but I have a good sense of direction and I ended up hitting Route 6 a few hundred feet east of the Snail Road intersection (my destination). From there I had to walk less than a mile to Ainsworth Cottages.

How's this for coincidence? As I walked on Route 6A toward the cottages, I saw three women walking. As I was uncertain about which way to go or how far to go, I said, "Pardon me. Could you direct me to Ainsworth Cottages?" One of the women replied, "I'm Ainsworth." She told me not only how to find her property, but in which cottage I could find Kip and René, that is, my cousin and his partner, whom, based on her comments and smile, she obviously adored. Later I met her husband, and thus I had let go of my thought that Linda Ainsworth and her two walking companions were lesbians. I'm starting to wonder if I am obsessed, in an unhealthy way, about sexual identity issues. Yet, at the same time, I know other people wonder and surmise about these things.

My visit with Kip and René was great. I got smiles and hugs, iced tea, sliced peaches and strawberries, and a piece of chocolate. I think it was a good idea to see them and be able to give them the map I copied, along with some instructions. They definitely plan to come to Thalassa tomorrow and bring lunch.

Monday, August 27 - 3:15 PM: I'm back atop the dunes in one of the Adirondack chairs. These are not really Adirondack chairs but rather homemade seats made with pieces of lumber. Beautifully situated over-looking the ocean, these chairs keep inviting me to come to them to read, write, and just look out and observe.

For lunch I had a bowl of the Scotch broth I made last week. I cooked a leg of lamb (from George and Kate, my Royalston farmer friends) for visitors a week ago—Howard Cruse, Ed Sedarbaum, Richard Goldstein, and Tony Ward. I used the bones, which yielded bits of meat for the soup, and added carrots, an onion from the garden, and barley. I mean, who eats barley? I really like it, yet rarely cook it. This is one of my favorite soups, and I loved having it here. A piece of home, like the glads and Cathy Stanton's very serious book. Who reads something like that on the beach? Me, I guess.

After lunch, I went down to the beach with a book and chair. I alternated between sunning myself (nude), swimming, and reading. I had to keep an eye out for the ranger's truck. He does pass through here, and nudity is not allowed. They give tickets. I supposed I could give a false name and address.

There's a rusty horseshoe nailed to the front of Thalassa, and I want to mention it partly because it is extremely rusty and perhaps has been there for decades. It means good luck, doesn't it? Well, I feel very lucky to be here. Is a mezuzah the same as a horseshoe? A religious version of good luck? I never considered putting either a horseshoe or a mezuzah on the Octagon, but now I'm considering it. I have a crescent moon from the Royalston Foundry (Jeff and Judy Bronnes' enterprise), a Celtic item I bought in Stratford, Ontario, and a friendship circle clay sculpture from Mexico or the American Southwest, a gift from Frederick and Stephen years ago. They bring me good luck already, but I suppose more would not hurt.

A small jet plane with U.S. Coast Guard markings flew by. Are such flights routine patrols around here? Looking for what? Nude sunbathers?

Monday, August 27 - 4:50 PM: The day remains clear with great visibility. I've used the house binoculars a few times, and I'm so appreciative. That's quite generous of the Trust or someone who donated them to Thalassa. I fetched four more gallons of water, a satisfying Thalassa chore. I seem to need eight gallons daily, which includes dishwashing, cooking, a shower, and filling the basin for a foot bath at the entrance to the cottage to minimize sand being tracked in. There are brooms and a dustpan, and I've already used them once.

I made some popcorn for the outhouse. It's not very good quality, and I won't be eating any. Unfortunately the twelve-ounce can of mixed nuts I brought with me is about two-thirds gone and it's only Monday. I'm going to have my steak dinner tonight. Why wait? I'm thinking of taking a nighttime beach walk, as the moon is almost full. I may walk in the dunes another night, but I'll have to stay on the Jeep trail or else I might get lost.

Monday, August 27 - 6:35 PM: I continue to walk out of the house frequently to stand atop the dunes and behold what is before me. The beach has been mostly deserted. I've seen individuals and couples walking just a few times and the occasional truck, Jeep, or van.

I saw someone walking on the beach a few minutes ago, and I noticed her long shadow. Then I spotted my own shadow about seventy-five feet to the east, on the slope of the dune. I raised both arms way in the air to make my shadow bigger. It immediately made me think of a photo I have of my friend Katya (formerly known as Nina) on a beach in Oregon, totally naked, arms raised in an expression of self-love or at least self-affirmation, and freedom, too, of course. I kept my shorts on, however.

Dinner was enjoyable but I have to say plain boiled cabbage, even with butter, is not my favorite vegetable, but it is green. I have the tea kettle on again.

Tuesday, August 28 - 9:00 AM: I didn't take my moonlight walk after all. I closed three of the five windows in Thalassa and went to bed instead. With the windows closed, the sound of the surf was muffled. The shack felt especially cozy. I slept well and arose with bright sunshine pouring in at seven o'clock. My morning routine was the same. I pumped four gallons of water and did the dishes.

I counted twenty-one boats out in the distance. A woman and her dog were on the beach. She was jogging, looked up and saw me, and we exchanged waves. The dog also looked up but didn't wave. A flock of thirteen gulls was at the shore when the jogger and her dog approached. Twelve gulls flew off together but one stayed behind. I wondered what made that gull behave differ-

Adirondack chairs and the beach

ently. As the jogger and dog got closer, that gull, too, went into flight. By then, its twelve former companions were nowhere in sight. Did the lone gull miss them? Would he find them later? I'll never know.

The air is crisp and the sky mostly blue with scattered cirrus clouds. I'm going for a walk on the beach. Kip and René said they'd be here around one o'clock.

Tuesday, Aug 28 - 10:35 AM: Last night's dew was amazing. Everything was very wet outside this morning, including items I'd hung out on the line. They're still wet. This morning's beach walk, about an hour long, was very enjoyable. I saw what I thought was a group of black birds resting on the water. As I got closer, I saw that they were a group of seals. A pod? I counted twelve of them. I think they were aware of my presence. A few of them made high pitched sounds, not very loud. What is it with the number twelve? Very Christian? Some of the seals dove beneath the surface and for a time there were seven, six, five, then back up they came.

A man approached driving a van towing a small boat. He stopped to look at the seals and he took out his binoculars. Since I didn't have mine, I approached him and asked for a look. He was quite friendly and made a joke about not liking to see seals. His "competition" for fish, I inquired, also asking him what he catches. "Anything," he said, "but I throw them back. I'm a sports fisherman." He said he likes coming here because it is peaceful and he can drink as much beer as he likes and nobody bothers him.

He asked me my age and said he'd already been coming here for four years when I was born. He told me he was seventy. He had white hair and a bandana on his head (red, white, and blue with stars and stripes). So I suppose his parents brought him here when he was a child, but I didn't get too inquisitive and he drove off. When I continued my walk, I saw him parked in the distance, then he turned around and, with a wave, drove past me again. I notice that various vehicles seem to do a lot of back and forth driving on the beach. Looking for just the right spot?

On the beach, I found a helium-filled Happy Birthday balloon, no longer with enough helium to stay aloft. I took it back to Thalassa and tied it to the birdhouse pole as a sort of joke. I can see why and how P-town artist Jay Critchley made art from beach detritus. I met Jay years ago, and we've exchanged emails now and then, but I don't look him up when I'm in P-town. Maybe I should have invited him to visit me in my dune shack. He is a P-town institution by now. Bill Murphy, my friend who lived here years ago, knows him. I suspect my friend John Magin of Truro, Roger Beatty's husband, knows him, too. I'll try to remember to ask John when I see him Saturday en route home.

There seems to be a lot of seaweed washing up today. I hope the swimming won't be unpleasant because of it. I'm going down to the beach now with book and chair.

Tuesday, August 28 - 6:50 PM: Another day draws to a close. Kip and René arrived at 12:55 and after some chatting, we had lunch outside. René put together wraps with hummus, turkey, and cheese. We also had sliced fresh peaches. After a while, we went to the beach. The seaweed was pretty bad, and I was the only one who took a swim. We saw a couple of seals. They stared at us, clearly observing us, but sudden movement on our part caused them to dive beneath the surface. The conversation ranged widely to cover family, work, friends, and lovers. Both guys are nature-lovers, especially René, and I encouraged them to visit Butterworth Farm.

I finished off the pasta for dinner and already had a cup of tea. Will I go for a moonlit walk? We shall see.

René Fontaine and Cliff "Kip" Bachner

Wednesday, August 29 - 8:15 AM: It's another beautiful late summer day. I didn't sleep as well last night, but still got plenty of rest. Having gone out to find Kip on Monday and having had the visit yesterday, I feel I have not experienced the solitude as strongly as I will from now until Saturday when I depart. And yet, I toy in my mind with the idea of hiking into town on Thursday or Friday. Maybe this intense amount of solitude is not for me. But if I go to town alone, will it be any different, even if the streets are covered with people?

Wednesday Aug 29 - 9:20 AM: I was seated in one of the Adirondack chairs atop the dune, listening to the surf. I finished Cathy's book and looked forward to talking to her about it. I did some mental comparison between her book, highly critical, analytical, and scholarly about Lowell and the National Historical Park, and on the other hand, my authorized and rather uncritical history of the Erving Paper Mills. We were working on our projects essentially at the same time but never discussed them. Of course, we had very different goals in these projects, but for both of us, inserting our personal values was important. Her work was scholarly. I was being paid by the paper mill owners to write an authorized history, but I was reassured I could maintain my values by focusing on the workers as much as management, and by dealing with difficult issues such as union organizing and river pollution.

The beach is truly deserted now except for some gulls lined up along the shore in a formation different from the usual flock bunched together. I can see about three seals just as I did yesterday. Do they ever come ashore to rest or for any other purpose? I can't imagine that they are in the sea a hundred percent of their lives like dolphins and whales, their marine mammal cousins. The sun feels very strong this morning and when I go down below I'll bring the beach umbrella. I have a new book to start, a 590-page novel by Ethan Mordden, en-titled *How Long Has This Been Going On?* which Curtis Graf chose for our Brattleboro gay men's book group. I've never read anything by Mordden, a gay writer of more than twenty books. Published in 1995, this novel is a saga about gay life from 1949 to the present, so the jacket copy says. I should be able to relate.

I did take a moonlit walk last night. The setting of the sun and the rising of the moon, pretty much simultane-ously, made for a dramatic, beautiful event out here in this near-wilderness setting. When I got down to the beach, I became a little concerned about finding my way back. Thalassa itself is not visible from the beach. The spot is easily marked by three poles sticking up from the dune's crest. Two of these have bird houses, but they were barely visible from the beach. I made note of some tire tracks, beach detritus, and footprints that would help. Even so, I chose not to take a very long walk, about thirty minutes only. A truck or van with bright headlights was discouraging, but at least there were no others. The full moon shining its light on the sand and dune grasses reflected in the water were mesmerizing. I walked close to the surf pounding the shore. Twice I heard a little chirp, but I didn't see any birds. I looked for the seals, but I didn't see them, either.

Wednesday, August 29 - 10:10 AM: For breakfast I sliced a peach and covered it with yogurt, specifically Stonyfield Farms plain whole milk yogurt. It was delicious. I recalled, as I occasionally do, the fact that for many years, I did not like yogurt, and specifically I remembered with so much regret my week in August 1968—all of thirty-nine years ago—at the Soviet-dominated World Youth Festival in Sofia, Bulgaria. Festival delegates were housed in college dorms and served meals in a large cafeteria. At breakfast, each place at the table was set with a large bowl and a server

photo by Bill Byrne

Seals on a sand bar

came by and ladled a generous serving of pure white yogurt. I had no idea at the time that for centuries Bulgaria has been famous for its yogurt. I just knew I did not have a taste for it. The server seemed both surprised and hurt when I declined the yogurt. And now I have regret after all these years.

Wednesday, August 29 - 12:50 PM: Thalassa suddenly comes into view as I make my way up the steep path from the beach. It's my home right now, and this seems amazing to me. I guess this is what it's like for the very rich who own not only a seaside home but a lot of land on all sides. Thalassa is so private and luxurious to me. I love all the chores—sweeping floors, washing dishes, hauling water. It's so basic and lovely. I'm reminded of the small rustic brookside Fern Cottage at Butterworth Farm and its current state of disrepair and disuse. I wish there were an easy answer to that, a simple way to fix it up and have it be used by someone who would appreciate it and enjoy the experience as much as I am enjoying this place called Thalassa.

On the beach this morning, before descending, I could see the seals so I took the binoculars with me. I was able to get a good look at these creatures, sleek and black and really quite large. The largest of them must weigh over two hundred pounds. I could see their whiskers and their large nostrils. A woman walked by, and we talked briefly about the seals. She said they are gray seals, and she's seen a group as large as thirty in this area. She said she does not know where they come onto the land. "They must do it somewhere," she said.

While I fetched water today, I ate about a dozen of the ripe purple beach plums. They tasted pretty good. They remind me of a Brazilian fruit, jaboticaba, which I enjoyed when I lived in Brazil in the 1960s as a Fulbright scholar. They're similar in size and color to Concord grapes but they have a single seed and grow in little bunches, more like cherries than plums. They grow on a small tree. I didn't pay any attention to the foliage. I'm not a very good botanist.

The Mordden book gets off to a good start, setting its opening scene in a gay bar in Los Angeles, 1949. But on the beach, reading became difficult because the biting flies are bad today, unlike yesterday when they didn't bother me and my two visitors. I try covering my legs with a towel, but the flies are tricky. I'll try to outsmart them with long pants, though that seems sad on a day like this. I want to go back to the beach and swim some more and continue reading. I took a swim earlier today and the seaweed problem is diminished.

I opened my second and last can of tuna for lunch (saved half of it for another day) and ate it with tomato and bread. I'm making sure I drink lots of water and keep some cold in the fridge, which works well. The *Living at Thalassa* booklet includes a "certificate of analysis" from Barnstable County Health Lab, based on a May 2006 water sample. No coliform, which is the most important thing, but it's high in sodium and has some discoloration or particles related to its iron content. Anyway, it's good enough for me to drink for a week, and it tastes OK, too.

Wednesday, Aug 29 - 6:35 PM: I enjoyed a long afternoon on the beach. It was very hot in the eighties, with bright sunshine and clear air. I was nude much of the time. Very few vehicles went by. A ranger went by after my shorts were back on. I set up a chair and umbrella closer to the dune, away from the seaweed being deposited by the waves, and thus I seemed to avoid the biting flies. I read on and off, staring into the distance. I counted more than thirty boats of different kinds, and often could hear their engines even though they were far away. Occasionally single-engine planes flew overhead. But I was very much alone and feeling OK, strong and healthy. I thought a lot about Dave, and I miss him, but it's also OK to be here without him. I should have told Kip to call him and report on our visit, but I thought of it too late.

For supper I finished the Scotch broth and the string beans and ate the next-to-last cuke. I want to try to catch the moon coming up in the east. That will happen in about half an hour. One way to ensure that I won't miss it is to go down to the beach and walk toward the east.

Wednesday, Aug 29 - 8:20 PM: My evening walk was great good exercise but my timing was a little off on the simultaneous sunset and moonrise. The sun set at 7:15 and the moon rose forty-five minutes later. It was big and yellow-red like the yolk of a farm-fresh egg. Anyway, I got to see and admire both on a one hour walk with no one on the beach but me, shore birds, and lots and lots of seaweed. This is my first journal entry by candle light. I don't know if it's enough for reading, but I also have my wind-up flashlight, which is very bright.

The Big Dipper, North Star, and Cassiopeia are right in front of me. I'm not much of an astronomer, but those I can readily identify. The Pilgrim Monument is nicely lit. I wonder if it and the Northampton City Hall were built around the same time as they both have that Italianate style which is not particularly common in New England. I'm going to have my second cup of tea for the evening.

Thursday, August 30 - 9:40 AM: I'm making popcorn for the shitter again. I think it's stupid. I can't see how a few ounces of popcorn are going to have a valuable composting effect. But I'll follow the instructions I've been given. *Living at Thalassa* mentions the possibility of mice and mosquitoes. Fortunately I haven't been bothered by mosquitoes, but today around five this morning, a mouse awakened me. I could hear it scratching somewhere. Was

Thalassa's clothesline and the author's towel with an environmental message

Bird footprints in the sand

it from inside or out? I've been fastidious about cleaning up, washing dishes, and leaving no food out. I'll put some popcorn on the three mouse traps if I remember.

It's another gorgeous day. As I went through the routines of using the outhouse and hauling water, I reminded myself that regularity is comforting as is the reliability of my well. These things seem so basic. Eat, drink, digest, eliminate waste. And without that supply of water, life here would hardly be possible at the rate of eight gallons a day, just for one person.

I didn't read for more than ten minutes last night. Candles and flashlight are not very practical. I went to bed and spent too much time obsessing over food and boredom. I considered going to town, but would I choose today (Thursday) or tomorrow (Friday) if I did? Would I eat lunch or dinner? Lobster at the Lobster Pot? Or maybe bluefish? I calculated and recalculated what I have left for food here, and it's just enough for my allotted time. Going to town is not likely for today, anyway. I think it would make me feel more lonely being among so many people I don't know. This adventure to town would end up being all about eating. Besides, I'm enjoying my new book. I'm making more of that infernal popcorn, and it isn't popping very well.

There are lots of birds flying around the dunes and the shack today, starlings, I think.

Thursday, August 30 - 12:15 PM: I stood naked on the beach for a while, no one in sight. I've been on beaches with relatively few people—Long Nook in Truro, for example—but never a place as deserted like this. What a feeling of freedom and self-awareness! The biting flies were pretty bad once I sat down to read, so I went back to the shack to get my long pants. Having outwitted the flies, I sat in the shade and read for a while.

I'm watching my food disappear, but it's not alarming as I am on schedule, and it's not as if I am in a wilderness. Lunch included the last of the tomato, the last of the tuna, and the next-to-last slice of bread. The nuts are gone. I could not ration them out until the end, as I hoped I would. It's all so basic—the food, the well, the outhouse, shower, garbage can. (I am taking the garbage out with me Saturday as required.)

Basic . . . and yet luxurious. How many people on earth can have this luxury, this comfort in such a beautiful place?

Thursday, August 30 - 5:35 PM: I just came in from my longest swim yet and my longest shower. The seaweed has diminished, and also I really needed to cool off.

I went on an expedition. Yes, I went to town after all. After lunch, I got horizontal and started to think about an outing that would include a strenuous walk across the beautiful (and sometimes eerie) dunes with a reward. Ice cream. And besides, I don't like rules, even ones I make for myself. Not that I really made any vow to be here solo for seven full days. As we used to say, "It's a free country!"

It took forty minutes to go across the dunes through the soft hot sand to get to Route 6, then about five minutes to the Cape Inn on Route 6A, where a shuttle bus took me to the town center. The fare was a dollar. The driver was Eastern European, like summer workers everywhere, and he was not helpful answering questions posed by me and others. When I got to town at three, a ferry was unloading, and scores of homos with baggage on wheels were arriving in town. The streets were crowded with gay men and lesbians and hetero tourists. I went to Joe's for a café latte then Ben & Jerry's for ice cream. I spent exactly an hour in town. There are lots of shows on at night, including Kate Clinton, whom I admire, respect, and find funny, too; Naked Boys Singing; and even Jeff Stryker, a one-time porn star who always fancied himself a singer, too.

At four, I took the shuttle out and trod through the sun-drenched dunes, stopping to drink water and shake the sand out of my shoes. Thalassa, with its peacefulness, was a welcome sight, and I quickly headed for the ocean where I saw a lone seal nearby but not so near as to scare me. (Those seals are HUGE.) I loved my expedition, and I'm happy to be back here. A huge flock of birds, swallows, I think, flew around Thalassa when I arrived and continued their swirling about as I poured two gallons of cool water into the solar shower to prevent scalding. I'd guess a count of two hundred birds in the flock. There's a nice breeze out which made my walk across the dunes more pleasant, and maybe the birds have a way of taking advantage of the air currents.

Today is Jordan Rosenfeld's birthday. He'd be twenty-three, I think, if his life hadn't been shortened by a car wreck. I'm thinking of him today and of my dear friends, Sam and Sacha, who suffer this loss (their only child) daily anyway, but I'm certain this day is especially painful for them. Dave and I look forward to seeing them this winter when we take a car trip to Florida. I trimmed the gladiolas again today, and I'll think of them today as flowers in memory of Jordan. Of course, the flowers Jordan liked best, *cannabis sativa,* no longer grow in my garden as my friends know. So I'll smoke some of the sacred herb in his memory, too.

Friday, August 31 - 9:40 AM: The weather changed as it always does. I'm fogged in, with visibility no more than a few hundred feet. I expected this based on what was happening last evening with clouds moving in and dramatic heat lightning to the northwest.

Dinner last night consisted of the leftover chicken, egg noodles, an onion sautéed in butter, and a splash of yogurt on top. I forgot to cook the cabbage or cauliflower, so I have both for today. Yawn.

After dinner, I went out to watch the moon rise. The night before, it rose at eight, and I went out a little before eight. I wanted to see the first glimmer of it, and I expected it would be perhaps five minutes later than the previous night. I waited a full twenty-five minutes before anything happened, and though the evening breeze was nice and I had my blue Land's End cotton sweater on, I got pretty impatient. Finally, I saw a white stripe of cloud brighten up, but it was another ten minutes before the yellow moon began to peek above the horizon. I don't know why, but I said out loud, "Hello, Moon." And at that moment I thought of my friend Moon Morgan, who probably was not named Moon by his parents.

I was in bed at nine, candles out, and had a little trouble falling asleep. I think I got entwined in many private thoughts and ideas.

I awoke at 5:30 AM to the sound of a mouse, but the sound stopped and I slept another two hours. By then it was all mist and fog with a slight chill. I closed some of the windows and made breakfast of yogurt, a peach that René and Kip left for me, and a cup of hot tea. I read a bit and hauled eight gallons of water from my reliable well. And, I'm popping more popcorn in anticipation of—well, you've heard enough of that. Will it rain? What's the weather back home? Today is my last full day and night at Thalassa. It's been great, and I'm still enjoying my book, but I'm ready to go home.

Friday, August 31 - 11:10 AM: The fog has lifted, but the sky remains about ninety percent clouded. I see bits of blue. There's one vehicle on the beach in the distance, otherwise quiet and empty. No seals in sight. Nor swallows or even gulls. Where have they gone?

photo by Allen Young

Thalassa, dune grass, rosa rugosa, *and the Atlantic Ocean*

There are some things in Mordden's saga that are annoying me. The chapter I'm reading is set in 1969 and the guys are talking about "circuit boys" and a big private "Red party" and having a gay liberation dance with cops and their wives invited. In 1969? No way. True, this is a novel, but a novelist has to be true to the times. No electric lights in *Gone with the Wind*. The almost tribal "circuit parties" were so named because enthusiasts of the frenzied and drug-induced dance marathons sometimes traveled to get to them in places such as Miami, New York, Palm Springs, and Montreal—often with color themes telling participants what to wear. These gatherings were a phenomenon that began in the late 1980s. Police departments and the gay community did not begin to develop positive relationships until at least a decade after the 1969 Stonewall Rebellion.

Friday, August 31 - 3:40 PM: I'm having a good day reading and checking the outdoors from time to time. The fog has returned, and I'm still wondering if we'll have an actual rainfall or storm, because the wind is picking up. I loved all the beautiful sunny weather I had, but it's also good to experience this—a little.

The *Living at Thalassa* booklet instructs me I must defrost the freezer the day before I leave, and I'm obedient, but it's taking much longer than they said it would. I don't mind. It's not as if I have a busy schedule today. Twenty-four hours from now, I'll be on my way home.

Saturday, September 1 - 9 AM: The weather broke dramatically overnight. Strong winds blew away all of the moisture, and I awoke to sunny blue skies, fresh air, whitecaps on the Atlantic. There are still some gladiola blooms open, and I think I'll leave them for the new arrival. He, or she, will arrive with the van that comes to fetch me—at least that's the system. (When I arrived, however, no one was here, though I don't know why.)

I'm ready to "hit the road." I have a few more chores to do, and then I'll just read, check the gorgeous vista a few more times, and wait.

Thalassa, a home away from home

Acknowledgments

The first person to read my Thalassa journal, when it was brand-new, was an old friend and longtime journal-keeper Katya Taylor. She said she liked it, which was one reason I moved forward with publication. She offered some editorial advice and lots of encouragement—and I'm always grateful for that.

I would also like to thank Sharon Nault for typing up the handwritten journal and for helpful questions.

My cousin Clifford "Kip" Bachner is mentioned in the journal on two different days—once when I visited him in P-town and once when he and his partner René visited me at the shack. I was grateful for these contacts in 2007 and am grateful now for his work on designing the cover for this book.

Giles Kotcher acted as a volunteer research assistant, not at my request, but because he was intrigued by the Provincetown scene and wanted to help. When I told Giles, whom I have known since we were both active in the New York Gay Liberation Front in 1970 and 1971, that I was working on an introduction for the publication of my Thalassa journal, he came up with many ideas and facts for me to think about. With political acumen as well as a scholarly and literary bent, Giles used Google and various public libraries in the Boston area to assist me. He found many websites and books with information, especially concerning the fascinating assortment of people I have written about in the introduction. His contribution to my understanding of Provincetown as a unique community is significant.

My sister Diane, my partner Dave, and my neighbors on Butterworth Road in Royalston, Massachusetts, where I enjoy my woodland home, offer welcome support just about every day.

Special thanks go to Marcia Gagliardi, proprietor of Haley's, who is my publisher, colleague, and fellow citizen of the North Quabbin region, for all she has done to help make this book better and the world more just, beautiful, and peaceful.

I have dedicated this book to the memory of Roger Beatty of Truro, a skilled and dedicated naturalist and educator who taught me a lot as we hiked various times in the Cape Cod National Seashore.

About the Author

Allen Young has lived in Royalston, Massachusetts, since 1973, coming with several friends to the North Quabbin Region of Central Massachusetts as part of the back-to-the-land movement. He helped build his own octagonal timber-framed house, has hiked and canoed throughout the region, and has cultivated a productive organic vegetable garden.

He first experienced forests, waterfalls, and gardening during his childhood on a poultry farm in the foothills of the Catskill Mountains in New York State,

photo by Diane Keijzer

Allen Young

where he was born in 1941. After graduating from Fallsburgh Central High School, he attended Columbia College in New York City, receiving the bachelor of arts degree in 1962. He earned a master of arts degree in Hispanic-American and Luso-Brazilian studies from Stanford University in California and a master of science degree from the Columbia University Graduate School of Journalism.

Upon receiving a Fulbright Scholarship in 1964, he spent three years in Brazil and other Latin American countries, contributing numerous articles to the *New York Times,* the *Christian Science Monitor,* and other periodicals.

Returning to the United States in 1967, he worked briefly as a reporter for the *Washington Post*, resigning in the fall of that year to become a full-time anti-war activist and staff member of Liberation News Service. In 1970, following the Stonewall Rebellion in New York City, Young participated in the gay liberation movement, collaborating with lesbian writer and scholar Karla Jay on four books, including the pioneering anthology *Out of the Closets: Voices of Gay Liberation.*

After returning to his rural roots, Young became a reporter for the *Athol Daily News*, later serving as assistant editor. He launched Millers River Publishing Co. in 1983 to produce his regional guidebook *North of Quabbin*, and published more than a dozen titles after that. Haley's published his *North of Quabbin Revisited* in 2003. From 1989 to 1999, he was the director of community relations for Athol Memorial Hospital. He was a co-founder of the North Quabbin Diversity Awareness Group. In 1998, he was the first recipient of the North Quabbin Community Coalition's Barbara Corey Award "in honor of his passion for life, his values and his love for the citizens of our region." In 2004, he received the Writing and Society Award from the University of Massachusetts English Department "honoring a distinguished career of commitment to the work of writing in the world."

He has served in Royalston town government on various boards and is chair of the town's Democratic Committee. He is a volunteer for the Mount Grace Land Conservation Trust, including many years as a member of its board of directors.

Young considers himself semi-retired, and continues to enjoy gardening and travel, as well as writing. His column, "Inside / Outside," appears weekly in the *Athol Daily News.*

The text and captions for *Thalassa* are set in Century Schoolbook. Century refers to a family of type faces derived from the original Century Roman cut by American Type Founders' designer Linn Boyd Benton in 1894. The typeface endures in the twenty-first century for periodicals, textbooks, and literature. The faces are noted for their exceptional legibility, so much so that the Supreme Court of the United States requires that briefs be typeset in Century family type.

Thalassa's titles are set in Gill Sans. Gill Sans is a humanist sans-serif typeface designed by Eric Gill. The original design appeared in 1926 when Douglas Cleverdon opened a bookshop in his home town of Bristol, where Eric Gill painted the fascia over the window in sans-serif capitals that would be later be known as Gill Sans. Gill further developed it into a complete font family after Stanley Morison commissioned the development of Gill Sans to combat the families of Erbar, Futura, and Kabel which were being launched in Germany during the latter 1920s. Gill Sans was later released in 1928 by Monotype Corporation.

a guide to nine Massachusetts towns north of Quabbin Reservoir
Athol • Erving • New Salem • Orange • Petersham
Phillipston • Royalston • Warwick • Wendell

Don't miss Allen Young's indispensable guidebook to the
North Quabbin region of central Massachusetts

NORTH OF QUABBIN REVISITED
ISBN: 1-884540-63-5 $22.95

Available from amazon.com and from the publisher,
Haley's • haley.antique@verizon.net

CPSIA information can be obtained at www.ICGtesting.com
Printed in the USA
BVOW07s2004220714

359996BV00001B/20/P